A Christian's Guide to KIPLING

A Woefully Inadequate Selection of the Works of Rudyard Kipling

Copyright © 2017

All rights reserved. This book or any portion thereof may not be reproduced or used in any manner whatsoever without the express written permission of the publisher except for the use of brief quotations in a book review.

Printed in the United States of America
First Edition, First Printing, 2017
ISBN: 978-1-945774-09-6

Trust House Publishers
P.O. Box 3181
Taos, NM 87571

www.trusthousepublishers.com

Ordering Information: Quantity sales. Special discounts are available on quantity purchases by churches, associations, and others. For details, contact the publisher at the address above.

Orders by U.S. trade bookstores and wholesalers. Please contact the publisher:
Tel: (844) 321-4202

1 2 3 4 5 6 7 8 9 10

Table of Contents

Poetry: The Supreme Art 1

The Life and Times of Rudyard Kipling 7
Kipling's India 7
Kipling's Life 13
Kipling's Legacy 21

The Poems 27
New Lamps for Old 29
The Gods of the Copybook Headings 31
Sestina of the Tramp-Royal 33
The Explorer 35
An Imperial Rescript 39
Mandalay 43
Sussex 45
Tommy 49
Soldier, Soldier 51
Tomlinson 53
Boots 59
Bill 'Awkins 61
En-dor 63
My Boy Jack 65
Cold Iron 67
Recessional 69

Poetry: The Supreme Art

Why Christians Should Read Poetry

Dr. Randy White

I'm not the first to suggest that poetry is the supreme art. Philosophers and common-folk alike have come to this simple conclusion. One may prefer the art of the canvas created with paintbrush or camera, or the art of sculpture created with clay, wood, or stone, but I'm not talking about preference. I'm talking about the art that reigns supreme. I believe that this is the art of poetry.

There are other word-based arts, of course. I regularly practice the art of oratory through preaching. It is a combination of the spoken word and (hopefully) sound logic. I also frequently make use of the art of rhetoric in the written word, which is somewhat more limited in persuasive ability than oratory. The sights, sounds, and immediate feedback from oratory outshine the written word on almost every occasion. Most of us love drama, in varying degrees, and drama is certainly a word-based art. But drama requires a stage, an actor, a script, and, more often than not, a cast.

Poetry, on the other hand, has the power of the spoken word, though it is written on paper. In this way, it reaches beyond its two-dimensional limitations. Poetry can capture the imagination like drama, but, unlike drama, it is portable. Poetry guides the mind, skillfully and painlessly, to a new vista of thinking. It can capture in words what we thought words could not capture. Unlike the novel, it does not require hundreds of pages. Poetry gets to the point and never lingers too long. Poetry is like an invisible hand that guides you to the "ah ha!" moment and, then, is mysteriously gone but never forgotten.

I haven't always liked poetry, and I still don't like all poetry. Too many poems are no more than syrupy sweetness. Other poems are just a series of rhyming words with no real depth. But, now and then, a poet comes along who has the power to see it, say it, and indelibly print it in our minds.

Anyone who remembers the Space Shuttle Challenger tragedy also remembers the words of President Reagan, spoken to the nation on the evening of the disaster. He spoke of the astronauts who "slipped the surly bonds of earth, and touched the face of God," using the words of John Magee, Jr.'s poem, "High Flight." I have no doubt that the President's words would have long been forgotten had he not captured the heart in these few, bright, vivid words.

Years ago, when traveling to Eastern Europe to engage in

witnessing opportunities by teaching English for two weeks, I was surprised when our host told us that we would have a poetry night. I thought, "How insane! We can't allow adults to stand in front of a group of other adults and recite poetry. They will think we're crazy!" However I quickly learned that I had travelled to a society that valued the art of poetry. When the poetry night came, all of their friends and family came out, packed the room, and listened with delight as the students recited poetry in English.

But our American society has outgrown poetry, it seems. We have come to think of poetry as "unmanly" (though we've been sissified in almost every other aspect of life). As a Christian, a pastor, and a thinker, I think Christians need to revive the love for poetry. I even think it would make us better Christians. Here is why:

We are people of "the Book." The Book, of course, is the Bible. The Bible is a book of words, which we call the Word of God. Not only is the Bible itself filled with large portions of poetry (there is even a section we call "the poetic books"), but also, if we read poetry we will become better readers of words themselves. We will learn to savor the words, to feast on them. And this is what we are to do with the Word of God. Diligent poetry readers are quicker to understand the Bible than non-poetry readers.

We are witnessing people. Christians have good news and want to share it. But we're not always good at sharing it. And, many of the sharing opportunities that we do have come in short bursts rather than in 30-minute time-slots with everyone seated neatly and quietly in the pew of a Sunday morning service. We have a few seconds here and a minute or two there in which a conversation is open to a witnessing opportunity. I believe that Christians will be far better equipped to capture the essence of our faith in a few, short, meaningful phrases if they are regular readers of poetry.

We are logic people. Much of the Christian world has left logic behind and fallen headlong into what I unpretentiously call the "stupid-trap." This is a trap that ignores facts and follows feelings. It is the trap that gets us worked into a trance or stirred into a frenzy, but has no caloric value. Good poetry is the art of mixing feeling with fact. Good poetry insists on sound, well-stated logic—which is exactly what the church needs more of today.

I hope you'll become a poetry reader. You may, like me, fall in love with the words and thoughts of Kipling. He was neither saint nor theologian, and I'm certain I wouldn't invite him to teach a Sunday School class. But he was insightful and a master of words, which is why he remains the youngest Nobel Laureate in history. Whoever your favorite poet becomes, I hope you'll gain a favorite. I hope you'll find one who challenges the mind and helps liberate it from dangerous ideas you didn't even know were there. I hope poetry helps you read better, interpret better, and even understand and communicate the truths of God better.

The protagonist of Kipling's *"The Explorer"* heard the words of the collective "they" that stop most of us from following our heart, but the explorer ignored those words and pressed on to brave new worlds. May poetry take you on such an expedition.

"THERE'S no sense in going further—it's the edge of cultivation,"
So they said, and I believed it—broke my land and sowed my crop—
Built my barns and strung my fences in the little border station
Tucked away below the foothills where the trails run out and stop

It's just the beginning of the tale, written in poetic form. And I hope you'll find the rest (it's included in this collection) and press on. Even if you don't keep any of the findings (barring samples)[1] you'll have the contentment of knowing that your mind (if not your body) went on the journey.

---

1 "Barring samples," a humorous line from Kippling's *The Explorer*. **1898**.

The Life and Times of Rudyard Kipling

Dillon Grahn

Kipling's India

Whatever one may think of imperialism in general, or of British Colonial India in particular, it would be impossible to fully understand Rudyard Kipling without understanding the nation into which he was born and which so captivated his heart and soul. And to understand India, it is necessary to understand the British Raj, or colonial rule.

Even some of the most outspoken detractors of the colonialist philosophy have had to admit that British rule in particular carried with it many benefits for the nations and societies so colonized; and this was perhaps especially true in the case of British India.

While it would be naïve to claim colonialism to have been an unmixed blessing to the native population of India, it cannot be denied that much good and little harm was wrought by the British Raj. In an 1871 speech on the benefits of British rule, Indian statesman and political leader Dadabhai Naoroji concluded:

> To sum up the whole, the British rule has been: morally, a great blessing; politically, peace and order on one hand, blunders on the other; materially, impoverishment, relieved as far as the railway and other loans go.... Our great misfortune is that you [the British rulers] do not know our wants. When you will know our real wishes, I have not the least doubt that you would do justice. The genius and spirit of the British people is fair play and justice.[2]

Ultimately, it would be British rule that saw India herself refashioned as a single, unified society. The challenges met and overcome by British engineers brought about an extensive network of railroads and paved highways throughout the various Indian provinces. At the same time, schools and industries were established, and improved medical, agricultural, and manufacturing techniques were introduced.

The governmental apparatus of the British Raj was largely staffed and operated by Indians, even exclusively so in some provinces. These local governors functioned harmoniously with the British authorities, and for perhaps the first time, the numerous and relatively isolated provinces of the Indian empire became a coherent nation with a common tongue and a shared culture. As a result, India saw increases in population, life expectancy, standard of living, education, and technology.

In this system, the British and native cultures remained separate

---

2 Naoroji, Dadabhai. "The Benefits Of British Rule (1871) - Internet History Sourcebooks".Legacy.fordham.edu. N.p., 1998. Web. 8 June 2016.

and profoundly distinct from one another; but they were not isolated. They interacted with one another directly on a daily basis and were deeply familiar with one another, all the while without falling victim to the naïve and erroneous assumptions of modern multiculturalism. Anglo-Indian[3] children spent the first years of their lives in the care of native nannies and teachers; young Kipling's first and preferred language as a child and as a young man was not English, but Hindi, and he spoke it with the fluency of a native.

On another note, the nearly two hundred years of British control of the Indian subcontinent certainly represents that region's longest sustained experience of Christian culture, although evangelism in India is traditionally dated all the way back to A.D. 52 with the supposed arrival of the Apostle Thomas. Today, there remain a few strongholds of Christianity in India, comprising approximately 2.3 percent of the population, but the vast majority of the population has rejected the faith. Indeed, one writer has rightly observed that "India has mostly passed up Christianity, and … there is no other country in the world that has proven so resistant and so impervious to it as India."[4]

Nevertheless, many of the institutions of western culture and government remain intact in modern India, though the Raj was terminated in 1947. British rule has left an indelible mark on the face of India, bringing that nation by main strength out of the middle ages and into the modern world, in which she now operates competitively

---

[3] "Anglo-Indian" was the general term for the English population of British India

and well, being one of the most successful and populous nations in the Orient. But England, forgetting or denying the great value of the colonial experience for the people of India, has done nothing in the intervening years but apologize for ever setting foot in India in the first place.

* * *

The history of British presence on the Indian subcontinent is a long and complicated one. We can trace the beginnings of that presence back to the sixteenth century, when British merchants began plying the trade winds east of Africa. The Portuguese explorer, Vasco da Gama, who sailed around the Cape of Good Hope and arrived at India in 1497, had already established sea trade between Europe and the Orient. This effectively broke up the absolute monopoly on Oriental trade, which had previously been enjoyed by Muslim merchants bringing goods by caravan across the Middle East.

In 1595, Dutch merchantmen first made their way into the Far East to establish their own trade with what is now Indonesia. That expedition was hugely successful, and the Dutch soon dominated the spice trade with the East Indies, becoming a colonial super-power in their own right.

It was in December of 1600 that Queen Elizabeth I granted a Royal Charter to "The Governor and Company of Merchants of London Trading into the East Indies," better known as the East India Company. This charter granted the EIC exclusive trading rights (among British merchants) in the Eastern hemisphere, from the Cape of Good Hope all the way to the Straits of Magellan, at the southern extremity of South America.

Although the initial destination of the East India Company had been the spice islands of Indonesia, the Dutch mercantile navy was already firmly established in that region, and after a few unsuccessful skirmishes with the Hollanders, the EIC turned instead to India in search of easier gains.

In 1614, King James I undertook diplomatic proceedings with Moghul Emperor Nur-ud-din Mohammad Salim, seeking to cement the trade presence of the British Empire in the Orient. The King's ambassador, Sir Thomas Roe, was eventually successful in gaining the Emperor's blessing on the East India Company to form a permanent base of operations in India. In 1617, Salim wrote the following in a letter to James I:

> "I have given my general command to all the kingdoms and ports of my dominions to receive all the merchants of the English nation as the subjects of my friend; that in what place soever they choose to live, they may have free liberty without any restraint; and at what port soever they shall arrive, that neither Portugal nor any other shall dare to molest their quiet; and in what city soever they shall have residence, I have commanded all my governors and captains to give them freedom answerable to their own desires; to sell, buy, and to transport into their country at their pleasure.
>
> For confirmation of our love and friendship, I desire your Majesty to command your merchants to bring in their ships of all sorts of rarities and rich goods fit for my palace; and that you be pleased to send me your royal letters by every opportunity, that I may rejoice

in your health and prosperous affairs; that our friendship may be interchanged and eternal."[5]

At this point, the company took up residence on the Indian subcontinent and began to build factories and permanent settlements, guarding those assets with armed troops.

* * *

The latter half of the seventeenth century was a troubled time for England. During this time, the nation was torn by civil war; King Charles I was deposed and beheaded by the parliamentarians; the monarchy was abolished and subsequently restored; and Charles II donned his father's crown. Yet through all of this, the position of the East India Company was only strengthened and solidified. So much so that, by the 1670's, Charles II had granted the company autonomy to hold and govern Indian territories, mint money, levy taxes, form alliances, raise armies, and make war and peace as it saw fit.

This prompted heavy resistance from the Indian empire, now allied with England's political foes, the French. Nevertheless, despite heavy setbacks, the EIC not only maintained its foothold in India, but increased its military capabilities, such that by the 1750's, the company's private army had expanded from a few hundred security troops to several thousand regular soldiers. In 1757, EIC forces achieved a decisive victory at Palashi and effectively took control of

---
5 The Great Moghul Jahangir. "Letter to James I, King of England, 1617 A.D." Letter. 1617. *Indian History Sourcebook: England, India and the East Indies 1617 AD*. Fordham University, 1998. Web. 7 Feb. 2016.

the Indian subcontinent. Company Rule in India lasted for a full century, until the Government of India Act of 1858 dissolved the East India Company and transferred the government of India to the Crown of England, then held by Queen Victoria.

* * *

In marked contrast with the East India Company, who had as little conversation with the native population as possible and had no interest whatsoever in nation-building, the Anglo-Indian population of the Raj was deeply involved in the interests of British India. The sub-continent was a treasured possession of the Empire, and the families who took up residence there had a deep love for their adoptive homeland. Nowhere is this in greater evidence than in the writings of Rudyard Kipling; his stories and poems are unanimous in testifying of their author's fervent love for the land in which he spent the most significant years of his life.

Kipling's Life

Joseph Rudyard Kipling was born on the 30th of December 1865, in Bombay, India, to John Lockwood and Alice MacDonald Kipling. He was named after Rudyard Lake in Staffordshire, England, where his parents met and courted. He spent his earliest years in Bombay, where Lockwood Kipling served as Principal and Professor of Architectural Sculpture at the Sir Jamsetjee Jeejebhoy School of Art.

When he was five, as was customary among Anglo-Indian

families, he and his younger sister, Alice, were sent to a boarding school in Portsmouth, England. Later in life, Kipling would describe the school as a prison-house, recalling the six years he spent there as a time of "calculated torture."

In 1878, he moved to another boarding school, this time the United Services College, in Devon. Although this school was intended to prepare boys for military service, young Rudyard's poor eyesight and general lack of athleticism precluded him from a career in the army. It was here, however, that he began to develop his literary abilities and accomplishments, editing and writing for the school paper under the mentorship of school headmaster Crom Price.

Kipling sent a few poems, written during this time, home to India, where his father had them printed privately in 1881, under the title *Schoolboy Lyrics*. This would be the first publication in what went on to become a truly monumental literary career.

* * *

As his school years drew to a close, Kipling's family lacked the finances to put him through university, and Kipling himself lacked the academic ability to earn a scholarship, so arrangements were made for his return to India. His father now held a position as Principal at an art college in Lahore, in what is now Pakistan. In 1882, Lockwood Kipling was able to obtain a job for his son as assistant editor with a local newspaper, the *Civil & Military Gazette*.

The return to his native land had a profound effect upon Rudyard, now in his sixteenth year. In his autobiography, *Something of Myself*, he would say of his first few days back in India that "my English years fell away, nor ever, I think, came back in full strength."

In 1887, Kipling was transferred from his job at the *Civil and Military Gazette* to a better job with its larger sister newspaper, *The Pioneer*, headquartered in Allahabad, where he had more freedom of expression. It was during his time with these two newspapers that he began to become known for his poetry and for his short stories. Already, in his earliest published work, the signs of genius were becoming evident. Here we find him affectionately, but for all that no less bitingly, critical of the Anglo-Indian populace and government; here we find him sympathetic, but never ignorantly idealistic, towards the native peoples of his homeland; here again we find his love for the common fighting man of the British Army, his respect for the officers of that army, and his unfeigned, unflinching, and unalloyed devotion to the Crown and to the Empire.

Like much of the Anglo-Indian population and government, Kipling and his parents would journey to the mountain town of Simla, the summer capital of the British Raj, to escape the oppressive summer heat of the lowlands. The young journalist looked forward to these month-long sojourns in the Himalayan foothills with great anticipation and describes their pleasures in the highest of terms.

In 1889, Kipling decided to return to London to pursue a literary career. He left his post at *The Pioneer*, sold the rights to a number of his published works, and left India. His journey, however, was a leisurely and a circuitous one, travelling east through Burma, Singapore, China, and Japan, before landing in

San Francisco. From there, over a number of months, he made his way across the length and breadth of the North American continent in no particular order.

Kipling was determined that, during this his first visit to the United States, he must pay a visit to the great American author, Mark Twain, whom the young Anglo-Indian admired with the deepest respect. This resolution proved more difficult to achieve than he had first imagined, but at last, a weary and travel-stained young Rudyard Kipling rang the doorbell of the Langdon house in Elmira, New York. As he waited for a response, he later recalled, "It occurred to me for the first time that Mark Twain might possibly have other engagements than the entertainment of escaped lunatics from India, be they ever so full of admiration."[6]

Nevertheless, the two littérateurs visited for an entire afternoon, smoking and conversing on all manner of subjects. It was an event that both men would remember for many years, and each would write about in their respective memoirs. In a letter home to India, later published in *From Sea to Sea*, Kipling wrote of his excitement at that great meeting:

> "You are a contemptible lot, over yonder [in India]. Some of you are Commissioners, and some Lieutenant-Governors… and a few are privileged to walk about the Mall arm in arm with the Viceroy; but I have seen Mark Twain this golden morning, have shaken his hand, and smoked a cigar—no, two cigars—with him, and talked with him for more than two hours! Understand clearly that I do not despise

---

[6] Hughes, James "Those Who Passed Through: Unusual Visits to Unlikely Places" from *New York History*, Volume 91, Issue 2, Spring 2010, pp. 146-152.

you; indeed, I don't. I am only very sorry for you, from the Viceroy downward. To soothe your envy and to prove that I still regard you as my equals, I will tell you all about it."[7]

Twain, for his part, clearly developed a great respect for the younger man, both that afternoon and in the years that followed, as Kipling's became a household name across the globe. In his autobiography, the American wrote about their meeting:

"He was a stranger to me, and to all the world and remained so for twelve months; then he became suddenly known, and universally known. From that day to this he has held this unique distinction: that of being the only living person, not head of nation, whose voice is heard around the world as soon as it drops a remark; the only such voice in existence that does not go by slow ship and rail but always travels first-class—by cable."[8]

Twain further quipped that "…[Kipling] is a most remarkable man—and I am the other one. Between us, we cover all knowledge; he knows all that can be known, and I know the rest."[9]

* * *

Kipling then resumed his eastward journey, crossing the Atlantic in October of the same year. Upon his return to London, he discovered that he had become somewhat of a celebrity among the

---

[7] Kipling, Rudyard. *From sea to sea and other sketches: letters of travel.* New York: Doubleday, 1899

[8] Twain, Mark. *Autobiography of Mark Twain, Volume 2: The Complete and Authoritative Edition.* Berkley, Los Angeles, London: University of California Press, 2013.

[9] Ibid.

reading public. Building upon his newfound acclaim, the young author continued to write and publish poetry and short stories, as well as his first full-length novel, *The Light that Failed*. By 1892, Rudyard Kipling had overtaken Alfred, Lord Tennyson as England's favorite author.

Kipling was the first to write "serious poetry" in the vernacular of the British soldiery, around whom so many of his poems revolve. This new style, along with his intimate knowledge of the fighting man and his impressive prowess with the English language and its many dialects, lends his writing a visceral power that allows him to put his reader in the very boots of "Tommy Atkins" without being in any way demeaning of the infantrymen of the Empire.

> *We aren't no thin red 'eroes, nor we aren't no blackguards too,*
> *But single men in barricks, most remarkable like you;*
> *An' if sometimes our conduck isn't all your fancy paints,*
> *Why, single men in barricks don't grow into plaster saints;*
>   *While it's Tommy this, an' Tommy that, an' "Tommy, fall be'ind",*
>   *But it's "Please to walk in front, sir", when there's trouble in the wind,*
>   *There's trouble in the wind, my boys, there's trouble in the wind,*
>   *O it's "Please to walk in front, sir", when there's trouble in the wind.*[10]

In that year also, Kipling married Caroline Starr Balestier, the sister of Wolcott Balestier, an American author with whom he had collaborated on another novel, *The Naulahka*. Kipling had been travelling yet again, intending to spend Christmas of '91 in India with his parents. Hearing of Wolcott's sudden death, he changed his plans

---
10 Kipling, Rudyard, "Tommy", *Barrack-Room Ballads*, 1892,

and returned to England. He proposed to Caroline via telegram while on his way back, and they were wed in January of 1892. The two had met only a year before.

After a honeymoon in America and Japan, the Kiplings settled down in a small cottage in Vermont, near Caroline's childhood home. Their first child, Josephine, was born on the night of December 29th in the same year.

Already a well-established literary figure, and now a wealthy man into the bargain, Rudyard wrote some of his most successful and most enduring works during this time in America, including *Many Inventions*, *The Jungle Book*, *The Second Jungle Book*, *The Seven Seas*, and *Captains Courageous*.

* * *

In 1896, the Kiplings celebrated the birth of their second daughter, Elsie, but their idyllic Vermont life was coming to a close. World events had created heightened tensions between America and the British crown, and Kipling started to see an increased anti-British sentiment in American society. With talk of war circulating on both sides of the Atlantic, the family of four packed their belongings and returned to England.

Kipling's writing, still eminently popular, took on a more pronounced political tone, showcasing the author's sense of foreboding for the future of his beloved British Empire. Poems like *White Man's Burden* and *Recessional* came out of this era. They were controversial upon their publication, and remain so today, with critics decrying what they regarded as blatant imperialist propaganda and racism. The fashionable ideas of the day were incompatible with the virtues of the colonial era, and his popularity began to decline, at least among society elites.

Nevertheless, he continued in his new role as the "poet of the Empire," supporting in his way the various war-efforts of the time. During this time, he made a number of significant political connections and was held in high regard by the more conservative elements of the government.

As the First World War began, Kipling became an enthusiastic supporter of British involvement in that war, fomenting a public anti-German sentiment (it was he who coined the pejorative 'Hun' for the German people) and presenting military service as the proper place for young men.

He made use of his government connections to gain entrance for his son, John (born 1897), into the Irish Guard. Like his father, John Kipling suffered from poor eyesight and was unable to qualify for military service without that assistance. In September of 1915, at the age of 18, John Kipling was killed in action, along with over twenty thousand other young Englishmen at the battle of Loos, in France.[11] His final resting place has only been ascertained with any degree of certainty in January of 2016.

Kipling's poem *My Boy Jack*, written in the same year, is certainly an expression of this loss, although it is not directly about the death

---

11 Le Maner, Yves. "The Battle of Loos (25 September to 19 October 1915)" *Remembrance Trails of the Great War in Northern France*. Web. 08 Feb. 2016.

of John. The name Jack in the poem refers to "Jack Tar," the Tommy Atkins of the Royal Navy. It was published in 1916 as a poetic introduction to a story about the battle of Jutland. In a 1997 stage play of the same title (later adapted to film, starring Daniel Radcliffe), David Haig took the poem to be more directly about John Kipling, even going so far as to change his name to Jack Kipling.

In the years that followed his son's death, Rudyard Kipling continued to write, but never again with the same level of enthusiasm or success as in his earlier years. He became involved in the War Graves Commission, an organization that tended the unimaginable number of graves for the casualties of the Great War, and later those of the Second World War also. It was Kipling who selected the inscription on the headstones of the fallen: "Their Name Liveth for Evermore" or "'Known unto God" if the identity of the fallen soldier was unknown.

Kipling continued to write for the remainder of his years, including a two-volume history of the Irish Guard. He was a harsh and vocal critic of communism, and he never wavered in his advocacy for the glory and virtue of the British Empire.

Rudyard Kipling died on January 18th, 1936. He remains to this day the youngest Nobel Laureate for Literature, and the first Englishman to gain that distinction, winning the prize in 1907 for *The Jungle Book*.

Kipling's Legacy

The import, value, and merit of the corpus of Rudyard Kipling's published work cannot easily be summarized. As a master of the literary craft, he remains practically unequaled for skill. Few writers have had as significant or as lasting an impact on the literature and the language in which they wrote; few have escaped the confines of the literary elite and penetrated as deeply into the consciousness of general public; few are quoted as often by people who have never heard his name. George Orwell, who despised deeply both Kipling's writing and his thinking, had this to say of him: "Kipling is the only English writer of our time who has added phrases to the language."[12]

In 1941, T. S. Elliot issued a collection of Kipling's verse with an introductory essay in which he defended Mr. Kipling against his many critics. In it, he wrote that Kipling possessed

> "An immense gift for using words, an amazing curiosity and power of observation with his mind and with all his senses, the mask of the entertainer, and beyond that a queer gift of second sight, of transmitting messages from elsewhere… all this makes Kipling a writer impossible wholly to understand and quite impossible to belittle."[13]

Indeed, Elliot would go on to say that "no writer has cared for the craft of words more than Kipling."[14]

Were his greatness a mere matter of technical prowess in his chosen craft, however, it would be a simple thing to discard his work and his thought, keeping and repurposing at will only those clever turns of phrase

---

12 Orwell, George. "Rudyard Kipling." *Horizon* Feb. 1942
13 Elliot, Thomas Stearns. *A Choice of Kipling's Verse made by T. S. Elliot with an essay on Rudyard Kipling.* Faber & Faber, London 1941
14 Ibid.

which might happen to catch our fancy. Yet even so great a detractor as Orwell was both unable and unwilling to do so. In his singularly obtuse, un-insightful, and downright bitter 1942 essay on Kipling (at least partly intended as a response to Elliot), he grapples with the conundrum (as he considers it) of Kipling's continued relevance:

> "Kipling is in the peculiar position of having been a byword for fifty years. During five literary generations **every enlightened person has despised him**, and at the end of that time nine-tenths of those enlightened persons are forgotten and Kipling is in some sense still there.... Kipling *is* a jingo[15] imperialist, he is morally insensitive and aesthetically disgusting. It is [necessary] to start by admitting that, and then to try to find out why it is that he survives while the refined people who have sniggered at him seem to wear so badly."[16]

Indeed, so right was Orwell in this observation that, in the seven decades that have passed since he penned it, Kipling's position has remained almost exactly as described, while Mr. Orwell himself has, to a large extent, gone the way of so many other "enlightened persons," being remembered today as little more than a political satirist.

But the extraordinary greatness of Rudyard Kipling lies not in his wordcraft, as marvelous as that is, but in the fact that he was *right*. He was right about men, he was right about nations, and he was right about the course of history. He saw things as they really are, and he was able to communicate that sight to the minds and hearts of others.

When we read Kipling we do not encounter a grandiose vision

---

15 Jingoism: "extreme chauvinism or nationalism marked esp. by a belligerent foreign policy" —Merriam-Webster

16 Orwell, Op. Cit. — Bold emphasis added, Italics in original

of "how the world would be if only...." Rather, we see through his eyes the same world in which live and breathe from day to day. In reading Kipling, we see times and places far removed from our own, and we encounter them from a perspective that is not our own. Nevertheless, we recognize the world that Kipling saw, because it is ours. We see ourselves in his world because we *are* in it.

When he saw the glory of his beloved British Empire slipping into the shadows of evening, his passioned warnings were met only with mockery; when he chronicled the beauty and enchantment of exotic locales, when he told of the daily, wearisome grind of the enlisted man, or recounted the soul and psyche of distant peoples: to all these things the critics incessantly responded, and still respond: "It's pretty, but is it Art?"[17]

The fact remains, however, that with pen and ink Rudyard Kipling was able to plumb the depths of the human experience with a level of sagacity and insight that Orwell and his "enlightened persons" have never been able to grasp, let alone achieve. As Ms. Gerould pointed out in 1919 (specifically in comments referring to his poem *Sussex*),

> "**...people actually do feel as Kipling says they do.** He has always tended to serve (in his own phrase) the God of Things as They Are. Granted, for the sake of argument, that it would be good for you to love all men and all countries alike, that fact remains that you do not. If that is your duty, most decent people do not perform their duty; their fathers did not, and their children will not."[18]

---

17 Kipling, Rudyard. "The Conundrum of the Workshops" *The Scots Observer* Sept 13 1890

18 Gerould, Katherine Fullerton. "The Remarkable Rightness of Rudyard Kipling." *The Atlantic Monthly* Jan 1919. Web Mar 3 2016 — Emphasis added.

And that is, in point of fact, the core of the mystery that so baffled and aggravated Mr. Orwell; the mystery of Kipling's continued endurance, as generation after generation of liberal writers has slipped into obscurity.

And this should come as no surprise, for all liberal thought necessarily bears an expiration date: the progressive of yesteryear is the ignoramus of today. The thoughts of conservatives, on the other hand, have a staying power beyond their specific time and place, because they are founded not on the world as it is thought it should be, but on the world as it really is. The insights of a Kipling, a Burke, or a Shakespeare remain as insightful today as they were in their respective centuries, for the world does not change with the changing whims of man. Thus, while the historical context in which Mr. Kipling wrote has faded into the past, the fact remains and will remain unchanged that "people actually do feel as Kipling says they do."

Nevertheless, the sympathies of the world have shifted ever farther from the philosophy that upheld the greatness of Christian Europe in centuries past, and ever deeper into the cesspool of liberalism, as each successive generation strives to be at the leading edge of progressive thought. As an inevitable consequence of this shift, it has become increasingly fashionable to disregard and despise Kipling's writings (and all true conservatism) as mere posturing for an outmoded way of life.

Those of us, however, who would seek to know the real world, the world whose Creator God declared on the sixth day to be "very good;" those who would seek to understand and to live well in that world; we would do well, you and I, to read not only our God's Holy Word, but also the words of those men who have seen the world for what it is and told us what they have seen. Among the names of those men the name of Rudyard Kipling will always stand preeminent.

Ultimately, the enduring body of work left behind by this great poet of the British Empire tells its own story. Say what you will, but Joseph Rudyard Kipling is, and will remain, one of the most important, powerful, and captivating voices ever heard in the English language.

A Woefully Inadequate Selection of the Works of Rudyard Kipling

New Lamps for Old

First published in The Pioneer, *in 1889, during Kipling's stay in Allahabad, this has been one of my favorite poems since my first reading of it. Rarely, if ever, has there been as eloquent a critique of the progressive mindset — the mindset that grasps blindly for something new, always something new. The new, the untested, makes beautiful promises for the future, but "behold—the Spirit lies!"*

Kipling's conservatism comes through very clearly even in this early work, as he urges a cautious distrust for the promises of a new and better world around the corner of the latest innovation.

— *D.G.*

WHEN the flush of the new-born sun fell first on Eden's green and gold,
A Lying Spirit sat under the Tree and sang, 'New Lamps for Old!'
And Adam waked from his mighty sleep, and Eve was at his side,
And the twain had faith in the song that they heard, and knew not the Spirit lied.

They plucked a lamp from the Eden-tree (the ancient legend saith),
And lighted themselves the Path of Toil that runs to the Gate of Death;
They left the lamp for the joy of their sons, and that was a glorious gain,
When the Spirit cried, 'New Lamps for Old!' in the ear of the branded Cain.

So he gat fresh hope, and built a town, and watched his breed increase,
Till Tubal' lighted the Lamp of War from the flickering Lamp of Peace;
And ever they fought with fire and sword and travailed in hate and fear,
As the Spirit sang, 'New Lamps for Old!' at the change of the changing year.

They sought new lamps in the Morning-red, they sought new lamps in the West,
Till the waters covered the pitiful land and the heart of the world had rest
Had rest with the Rain of the Forty Days, but the Ark rode safe above,
And the Spirit cried, 'New Lamps for Old!' when Noah loosened the Dove.

And some say now that the Eden-tree had never a root on earth;
And some say now from an eyeless eft our Father Adam had birth;
And some say now there was never an Ark and never a God to save;
And some say now that Man is a God, and some say Man is a slave;

And some build altars East and West, and some build North and South;
And some bow down to the Work of the Hand and some to the Word of the Mouth.
But wheresoever a heart may beat or a hand reach forth to hold,
The Spirit comes with the coming year, and cries, 'New Lamps for Old!'

And the sons of Adam leave their toil who are cursed with the Curse of Hope,
And hang the profitless past in a noose of the thundering belfry's rope,
And tear the branch from the laurel-bush with feastings manifold,
When the cry goes up to the scornful stars, 'New Lamps! New Lamps for Old!'

Though all the lamps that ever were lit have winked at the world for years,
The sons of Adam crowd the streets with laughter and sighs and tears;
For they hold that new, strange lamps shall shine to guide their feet aright,
And they turn their eyes to the scornful stars and stretch their arms to the night.

And the Spirit gives them the Lamp of War that burns at the cannonlip,
As it blazed on the point of Tubal's blade and the prow of the battleship;
And the Lamp of Love that was Eve's to snatch from Lilith under the Tree;
And the Lamp of Fame that is old as Strife and dim as Memory;

And the Lamp of Faith that was won from Job, and of Shame that was wrung from Cain;
And the Lamp of Youth that was Adam's once, and the cold blue Lamp of Pain;
And last is the terrible Lamp of Hope that every man must bear,
Lest he find his peace ere the day of his death by the light of the Lamp Despair.

We know that the Eden Lamp is lost, —if ever were Eden made,
And the ink of the Schools in the Lamp of Faith has sunk a world in the shade;
But ever we look for a light that is new, and ever the Spirit cries,
'New Lamps for Old!' and we take the lamps, and—behold, the Spirit lies!

The Gods of the Copybook Headings

As a schoolboy, young Rudyard would have been intimately familiar with copybook headings. A simple phrase or maxim expressing some virtue of the Western world would be printed atop each page of the copybook, which students would copy down the length of the page in the practice of penmanship.

In this poem, published in 1919, Kipling picks up a concurrent theme to that of New Lamps for Old, *as the simple, eternal truths of reality outlast and overpower the wishful thinking of mankind.*

— D.G.

AS I PASS through my incarnations in every age and race,
I make my proper prostrations to the Gods of the Market Place.
Peering through reverent fingers I watch them flourish and fall,
And the Gods of the Copybook Headings, I notice, outlast them all.

We were living in trees when they met us. They showed us each in turn
That Water would certainly wet us, as Fire would certainly burn:
But we found them lacking in Uplift, Vision and Breadth of Mind,
So we left them to teach the Gorillas while we followed the March of Mankind.

We moved as the Spirit listed. They never altered their pace,
Being neither cloud nor wind-borne like the Gods of the Market Place,
But they always caught up with our progress, and presently word would come
That a tribe had been wiped off its icefield, or the lights had gone out in Rome.

With the Hopes that our World is built on they were utterly out of touch,
They denied that the Moon was Stilton; they denied she was even Dutch;
They denied that Wishes were Horses; they denied that a Pig had Wings;
So we worshipped the Gods of the Market Who promised these beautiful things.

When the Cambrian measures were forming, They promised perpetual peace.
They swore, if we gave them our weapons, that the wars of the tribes would cease.

But when we disarmed They sold us and delivered us bound to our foe,
And the Gods of the Copybook Headings said: "Stick to the Devil you know."

On the first Feminian Sandstones we were promised the Fuller Life
(Which started by loving our neighbour and ended by loving his wife)
Till our women had no more children and the men lost reason and faith,
And the Gods of the Copybook Headings said: "The Wages of Sin is Death."

In the Carboniferous Epoch we were promised abundance for all,
By robbing selected Peter to pay for collective Paul;
But, though we had plenty of money, there was nothing our money could buy,
And the Gods of the Copybook Headings said: "If you don't work you die."

Then the Gods of the Market tumbled, and their smooth-tongued wizards withdrew
And the hearts of the meanest were humbled and began to believe it was true
That All is not Gold that Glitters, and Two and Two make Four
And the Gods of the Copybook Headings limped up to explain it once more.

As it will be in the future, it was at the birth of Man
There are only four things certain since Social Progress began.
That the Dog returns to his Vomit and the Sow returns to her Mire,
And the burnt Fool's bandaged finger goes wabbling back to the Fire;

And that after this is accomplished, and the brave new world begins
When all men are paid for existing and no man must pay for his sins,
As surely as Water will wet us, as surely as Fire will burn,
The Gods of the Copybook Headings with terror and slaughter return!

Sestina of the Tramp-Royal

A sestina is a difficult poem to write. It has seven stanzas, the first six composed of six lines and the last of three. The last word of each line of the first stanza must be repeated as the last word of each line in the following stanzas, in a prescribed order. Below we use the alphabet to designate the prescribed order of the last words. The first stanza is ABCDEF, and the last word of the first line of the second stanza must be the word F from the first stanza.

Kipling only wrote one sestina, as far as we know. In it, he shows his masterful skill at language and his love for travel, as he describes a "Tramp-royal," who is always eager to move on to see a new corner of this world. This poem was written in 1896.

— R.W.

ABCDEF

Speakin' in general, I 'ave tried 'em all—
The 'appy roads that take you o'er the world.
Speakin' in general, I 'ave found them good
For such as cannot use one bed too long,
But must get 'ence, the same as I 'ave done,
An' go observin' matters till they die.

FAEBDC

What do it matter where or 'ow we die,
So long as we've our 'ealth to watch it all—
The different ways that different things are done,
An' men an' women lovin' in this world;
Takin' our chances as they come along,
An' when they ain't, pretendin' they are good?

CFDABE

In cash or credit—no, it aren't no good;
You 'ave to 'ave the 'abit or you'd die,

Unless you lived your life but one day long,
Nor didn't prophesy nor fret at all,
But drew your tucker some'ow from the world,
An' never bothered what you might ha' done.

ECBFAD
But, Gawd, what things are they I 'aven't done?
I've turned my 'and to most, an' turned it good,
In various situations round the world—
For 'im that doth not work must surely die;
But that's no reason man should labour all
'Is life on one same shift—life's none so long.

DEACFB
Therefore, from job to job I've moved along.
Pay couldn't 'old me when my time was done,
For something in my 'ead upset it all,
Till I 'ad dropped whatever 'twas for good,
An', out at sea, be'eld the dock-lights die,
An' met my mate—the wind that tramps the world!

BDFECA
It's like a book, I think, this bloomin' world,
Which you can read and care for just so long,
But presently you feel that you will die
Unless you get the page you're readin' done,
An' turn another—likely not so good;
But what you're after is to turn 'em all.

ECA (and inlude BDF)
Gawd bless this world! Whatever she 'ath done—
Excep' when awful long I've found it good.
So write, before I die, "E liked it all!"

The Explorer

Here is a poem of wonder and intrigue; the tale of an explorer who ventures beyond the place that the people had decreed to be the "edge of cultivation," where there was "no sense in going further." It's a poem about challenging the status quo, listening to your instinct, and not really caring whether you get the credit for your discoveries. The Explorer was written in 1898.

—*R.W.*

"THERE'S no sense in going further—it's the edge of cultivation,"
  So they said, and I believed it—broke my land and sowed my crop—
Built my barns and strung my fences in the little border station
  Tucked away below the foothills where the trails run out and stop.

Till a voice, as bad as Conscience, rang interminable changes
  On one everlasting Whisper day and night repeated—so:
"Something hidden. Go and find it. Go and look behind the Ranges—
  "Something lost behind the Ranges. Lost and waiting for you. Go!"

So I went, worn out of patience; never told my nearest neighbours—
  Stole away with pack and ponies—left 'em drinking in the town;
And the faith that moveth mountains didn't seem to help my labours
  As I faced the sheer main-ranges, whipping up and leading down.

March by march I puzzled through 'em, turning flanks and dodging shoulders,
  Hurried on in hope of water, headed back for lack of grass;
Till I camped above the tree-line—drifted snow and naked boulders—
  Felt free air astir to windward—knew I'd stumbled on the Pass.

'Thought to name it for the finder: but that night the Norther found me—
  Froze and killed the plains-bred ponies; so I called the camp Despair
(It's the Railway Gap to-day, though). Then my Whisper waked to hound me:—
  "Something lost behind the Ranges. Over yonder! Go you there!"

Then I knew, the while I doubted—knew His Hand was certain o'er me.
  Still—it might be self-delusion—scores of better men had died—
I could reach the township living, but ... He knows what terror tore me ...
  But I didn't ... but I didn't. I went down the other side,

Till the snow ran out in flowers, and the flowers turned to aloes,
  And the aloes sprung to thickets and a brimming stream ran by;
But the thickets dwined to thorn-scrub, and the water drained to shallows,
  And I dropped again on desert—blasted earth, and blasting sky....

I remember lighting fires; I remember sitting by 'em;
  I remember seeing faces, hearing voices, through the smoke;
I remember they were fancy—for I threw a stone to try 'em.
  "Something lost behind the Ranges" was the only word they spoke.

I remember going crazy. I remember that I knew it
  When I heard myself hallooing to the funny folk I saw.
'Very full of dreams that desert, but my two legs took me through it ...
  And I used to watch 'em moving with the toes all black and raw.

But at last the country altered—White Man's country past disputing—
  Rolling grass and open timber, with a hint of hills behind—
There I found me food and water, and I lay a week recruiting.
  Got my strength and lost my nightmares. Then I entered on my find.

'Thence I ran my first rough survey—chose my trees and blazed and ringed 'em—
   Week by week I pried and sampled—week by week my findings grew.
Saul he went to look for donkeys, and by God he found a kingdom!
   But by God, who sent His Whisper, I had struck the worth of two!

Up along the hostile mountains, where the hair-poised snowslide shivers—
   Down and through the big fat marshes that the virgin ore-bed stains,
Till I heard the mile-wide mutterings of unimagined rivers,
   And beyond the nameless timber saw illimitable plains!

'Plotted sites of future cities, traced the easy grades between 'em;
   Watched unharnessed rapids wasting fifty thousand head an hour;
Counted leagues of water-frontage through the axe-ripe woods that screen 'em—
   Saw the plant to feed a people—up and waiting for the power!

Well I know who'll take the credit—all the clever chaps that followed—
   Came, a dozen men together—never knew my desert-fears;
Tracked me by the camps I'd quitted, used the water-holes I'd hollowed.
   They'll go back and do the talking. They'll be called the Pioneers!

They will find my sites of townships—not the cities that I set there.
   They will rediscover rivers—not my rivers heard at night.
By my own old marks and bearings they will show me how to get there,
   By the lonely cairns I builded they will guide my feet aright.

Have I named one single river? Have I claimed one single acre?
   Have I kept one single nugget—(barring samples)? No, not I!
Because my price was paid me ten times over by my Maker.
   But you wouldn't understand it. You go up and occupy.

Ores you'll find there; wood and cattle; water-transit sure and steady
  (That should keep the railway rates down), coal and iron at your doors.
God took care to hide that country till He judged His people ready,
  Then He chose me for His Whisper, and I've found it, and it's yours!

Yes, your "Never-never country"—yes, your "edge of cultivation"
  And "no sense in going further"—till I crossed the range to see.
God forgive me! No, I didn't. It's God's present to our nation.
  Anybody might have found it but—His Whisper came to Me!

An Imperial Rescript

Kipling's 1890 poem, An Imperial Rescript, *is the German Kaiser's answer to the call of the working class to ease their burden. As a politician, he's got the answer to their burden, so he thinks. Calling together the notable officials from around the kingdom, the Kaiser leads them to a utopian (albeit socialist) solution to all their woes. Everyone gathered is ready to sign, encouraged by the enthusiastic cry of the proletariat. Suddenly, however, a laugh cries through the hall: the laugh of "Sadie, Mimi, or Olga, Gretchen, or Mary Jane," a list of names covering the gamut of ages and locales. From here, Kipling tells how the various delegates speak words of concern for their own personal wellbeing, a wellbeing that may be compromised by the Kaiser's socialist solution. In the end, Kipling conveys his point: socialism may be wonderful in concept, but it is brutal when it takes one's wealth and gives it to others.*

Kipling, with such poetic ease, communicates that capitalism is the only economic plan that will work, "till we are built like angels." He closes his poem with several references to literature (Biblical and otherwise) that speak of doing the impossible, such as "belling the cat" (Aesop's fable), "razoring the Grindstone," and getting "figs from thistles" (Matthew 7:16). The poem also mentions W. Hohenzollern, a historical reference to William Hohenzollern of the German royal family.

So, enjoy the poem. And forget about trying to do what has been done so many times before: "to ease the strong of their burden, to help the weak in their need." As Jesus said, "the poor you have with you always" (Matthew 26:11). Rather than trying to find some government, church, or denominational program that leads in a humanitarian "march to peace and plenty in the bond of brotherhood," just "work for the kids and the missus" (or, as Scripture puts it: "if anyone does not take care of his own, he is worse than an infidel"—1 Timothy 5:8).

—R.W.

Now this is the tale of the Council the German Kaiser decreed,
To ease the strong of their burden, to help the weak in their need,
He sent a word to the peoples, who struggle, and pant, and sweat,
That the straw might be counted fairly and the tally of bricks be set.

The Lords of Their Hands assembled; from the East and the West they drew —
Baltimore, Lille, and Essen, Brummagem, Clyde, and Crewe.
And some were black from the furnace, and some were brown from the soil,
And some were blue from the dye-vat; but all were wearied of toil.

And the young King said: — "I have found it, the road to the rest ye seek:
The strong shall wait for the weary, the hale shall halt for the weak:
With the even tramp of an army where no man breaks from the line,
Ye shall march to peace and plenty in the bond of brotherhood — sign!"

The paper lay on the table, the strong heads bowed thereby,
And a wail went up from the peoples: — "Ay, sign — give rest, for we die!"
A hand was stretched to the goose-quill, a fist was cramped to scrawl,
When — the laugh of a blue-eyed maiden ran clear through the Council-hall.

And each one heard Her laughing as each one saw Her plain —
Saidie, Mimi, or Olga, Gretchen, or Mary Jane.
And the Spirit of Man that is in Him to the light of the vision woke;
And the men drew back from the paper, as a Yankee delegate spoke: —

"There's a girl in Jersey City who works on the telephone;
We're going to hitch our horses and dig for a house of our own,
With gas and water connections, and steam-heat through to the top;
And, W. Hohenzollern, I guess I shall work till I drop."

And an English delegate thundered: — "The weak an' the lame be blowed!
I've a berth in the Sou'-West workshops, a home in the Wandsworth Road;
And till the 'sociation has footed my buryin' bill,
I work for the kids an' the missus. Pull up? I be shammed[19] if I will!"

And over the German benches the bearded whisper ran: —
"Lager, der girls und der dollars, dey makes or dey breaks a man.

---

19 word changed

If Schmitt haf collared der dollars, he collars der girl deremit;
But if Schmitt bust in der pizness, we collars der girl from Schmitt."

They passed one resolution: — "Your sub-committee believe
You can lighten the curse of Adam when you've lifted the curse of Eve.
But till we are built like angels — with hammer and chisel and pen,
We will work for ourself and a woman, for ever and ever, amen."

Now this is the tale of the Council the German Kaiser held —
The day that they razored the Grindstone, the day that the Cat was belled,
The day of the Figs from Thistles, the day of the Twisted Sands,
The day that the laugh of a maiden made light of the Lords of Their Hands.

Mandalay

••••●••••

Published in 1890, the restless feel of the meter and word-choice speaks of the enchantment that the East held for Kipling and of his visit to Burma on his journey back to England the year before. Mandalay *has long been one of his most famous poems, as its unassuming power draws the reader to a far and distant land as surely as if you had been there with the author. A few verses of the poem were adapted for music in 1907 by Oley Speaks, and were even recorded by Frank Sinatra in 1957.*

— D.G.

By the old Moulmein Pagoda, lookin' eastward to the sea,
There's a Burma girl a-settin', and I know she thinks o' me;
For the wind is in the palm-trees, and the temple-bells they say:
"Come you back, you British soldier; come you back to Mandalay!"
   Come you back to Mandalay,
   Where the old Flotilla lay:
   Can't you 'ear their paddles chunkin' from Rangoon to Mandalay?
   On the road to Mandalay,
   Where the flyin'-fishes play,
   An' the dawn comes up like thunder outer China 'crost the Bay!

'Er petticoat was yaller an' 'er little cap was green,
An' 'er name was Supi-yaw-lat — jes' the same as Theebaw's Queen,
An' I seed her first a-smokin' of a whackin' white cheroot,
An' a-wastin' Christian kisses on an 'eathen idol's foot:
   Bloomin' idol made o' mud —
   Wot they called the Great Gawd Budd —
   Plucky lot she cared for idols when I kissed 'er where she stud!
   On the road to Mandalay . . .

When the mist was on the rice-fields an' the sun was droppin' slow,
She'd git 'er little banjo an' she'd sing "Kulla-lo-lo!"

With 'er arm upon my shoulder an' 'er cheek agin' my cheek
We useter watch the steamers an' the hathis pilin' teak.
    Elephints a-pilin' teak
    In the sludgy, squdgy creek,
      Where the silence 'ung that 'eavy you was 'arf afraid to speak!
    On the road to Mandalay . . .

But that's all shove be'ind me — long ago an' fur away,
An' there ain't no 'busses runnin' from the Bank to Mandalay;
An' I'm learnin' 'ere in London what the ten-year soldier tells:
"If you've 'eard the East a-callin', you won't never 'eed naught else."
    No! you won't 'eed nothin' else
    But them spicy garlic smells,
      An' the sunshine an' the palm-trees an' the tinkly temple-bells;
    On the road to Mandalay . . .

I am sick o' wastin' leather on these gritty pavin'-stones,
An' the blasted Henglish drizzle wakes the fever in my bones;
Tho' I walks with fifty 'ousemaids outer Chelsea to the Strand,
An' they talks a lot o' lovin', but wot do they understand?
    Beefy face an' grubby 'and —
    Law! wot do they understand?
      I've a neater, sweeter maiden in a cleaner, greener land!
    On the road to Mandalay . . .

Ship me somewheres east of Suez, where the best is like the worst,
Where there aren't no Ten Commandments an' a man can raise a thirst;
For the temple-bells are callin', an' it's there that I would be —
By the old Moulmein Pagoda, looking lazy at the sea;
    On the road to Mandalay,
    Where the old Flotilla lay,
      With our sick beneath the awnings when we went to Mandalay!
    On the road to Mandalay,
    Where the flyin'-fishes play,
      An' the dawn comes up like thunder outer China 'crost the Bay!

Sussex

In a marked contrast to the wanderlust of Tramp-Royal, The Explorer, *or* Mandalay, *this 1902 poem shows the provinciality of a man at home. It is one of my favorite expressions of the Love of Place that has so largely been rejected by modern man. Here we find an unabashed and profoundly healthy joy and pride in the author's beloved country with no concomitant derogatory sense toward other locals.*

— D.G.

God gave all men all earth to love,
   But, since our hearts are small
Ordained for each one spot should prove
   Beloved over all;
That, as He watched Creation's birth,
   So we, in godlike mood,
May of our love create our earth
   And see that it is good.

So one shall Baltic pines content,
   As one some Surrey glade,
Or one the palm-grove's droned lament
   Before Levuka's Trade.
Each to his choice, and I rejoice
   The lot has fallen to me
In a fair ground-in a fair ground —
Yea, Sussex by the sea!

No tender-hearted garden crowns,
   No bosonied woods adorn
Our blunt, bow-headed, whale-backed Downs,
   But gnarled and writhen thorn —
Bare slopes where chasing shadows skim,

And, through the gaps revealed,
Belt upon belt, the wooded, dim,
Blue goodness of the Weald.

Clean of officious fence or hedge,
   Half-wild and wholly tame,
The wise turf cloaks the white cliff-edge
   As when the Romans came.
What sign of those that fought and died
   At shift of sword and sword?
The barrow and the camp abide,
   The sunlight and the sward.

Here leaps ashore the full Sou'west
   All heavy-winged with brine,
Here lies above the folded crest
   The Channel's leaden line,
And here the sea-fogs lap and cling,
   And here, each warning each,
The sheep-bells and the ship-bells ring
   Along the hidden beach.

We have no waters to delight
   Our broad and brookless vales —
Only the dewpond on the height
   Unfed, that never fails —
Whereby no tattered herbage tells
   Which way the season flies —
Only our close-bit thyme that smells
   Like dawn in Paradise.

Here through the strong and shadeless days
   The tinkling silence thrills;
Or little, lost, Down churches praise

     The Lord who made the hills:
But here the Old Gods guard their round,
     And, in her secret heart,
The heathen kingdom Wilfrid found
     Dreams, as she dwells, apart.

Though all the rest were all my share,
     With equal soul I'd see
Her nine-and-thirty sisters fair,
     Yet none more fair than she.
Choose ye your need from Thames to Tweed,
     And I will choose instead
Such lands as lie 'twixt Rake and Rye,
     Black Down and Beachy Head.

I will go out against the sun
     Where the rolled scarp retires,
And the Long Man of Wilmington
     Looks naked toward the shires;
And east till doubling Rother crawls
     To find the fickle tide,
By dry and sea-forgotten walls,
     Our ports of stranded pride.

I will go north about the shaws
     And the deep ghylls that breed
Huge oaks and old, the which we hold
     No more than Sussex weed;
Or south where windy Piddinghoe's
     Begilded dolphin veers,
And red beside wide-banked Ouse
     Lie down our Sussex steers.

So to the land our hearts we give
   Til the sure magic strike,
And Memory, Use, and Love make live
   Us and our fields alike —
That deeper than our speech and thought,
   Beyond our reason's sway,
Clay of the pit whence we were wrought
   Yearns to its fellow-clay.

God gives all men all earth to love,
   But, since man's heart is small,
Ordains for each one spot shall prove
   Beloved over all.
Each to his choice, and I rejoice
   The lot has fallen to me
In a fair ground-in a fair ground —
   Yea, Sussex by the sea!

Tommy

Leading up to and during World War I, a common soldier in the British Army was often referred to under the collective name, "Tommy Atkins." This is equivalent to G.I. Joe in World War II America. Tommy Atkins was, therefore, a name for the nameless thousands of soldiers in Imperial Great Britain.

Rudyard Kipling had a masterful ability to catch humanity at its best and, in this case, at its worst. In Tommy, the character of the solider is seen, and, even more strikingly, the character of the public, which admires Tommy in battle but despises Tommy in the community.

Kipling included Tommy *in* Barrack Room Ballads I, *written from 1889-1891, a collection in which Kipling expressed the deepest respect for the soldier.*

—R.W.

I went into a public-'ouse to get a pint o' beer,
The publican 'e up an' sez, "We serve no red-coats here."
The girls be'ind the bar they laughed an' giggled fit to die,
I outs into the street again an' to myself sez I:
    O it's Tommy this, an' Tommy that, an' "Tommy, go away";
    But it's "Thank you, Mister Atkins", when the band begins to play,
    The band begins to play, my boys, the band begins to play,
    O it's "Thank you, Mister Atkins", when the band begins to play.

I went into a theatre as sober as could be,
They gave a drunk civilian room, but 'adn't none for me;
They sent me to the gallery or round the music-'alls,
But when it comes to fightin', Lord! they'll shove me in the stalls!
    For it's Tommy this, an' Tommy that, an' "Tommy, wait outside";
    But it's "Special train for Atkins" when the trooper's on the tide,
    The troopship's on the tide, my boys, the troopship's on the tide,
    O it's "Special train for Atkins" when the trooper's on the tide.

Yes, makin' mock o' uniforms that guard you while you sleep
Is cheaper than them uniforms, an' they're starvation cheap;
An' hustlin' drunken soldiers when they're goin' large a bit
Is five times better business than paradin' in full kit.
    Then it's Tommy this, an' Tommy that, an' "Tommy, 'ow's yer soul?"
    But it's "Thin red line of 'eroes" when the drums begin to roll,
    The drums begin to roll, my boys, the drums begin to roll,
    O it's "Thin red line of 'eroes" when the drums begin to roll.

We aren't no thin red 'eroes, nor we aren't no blackguards too,
But single men in barricks, most remarkable like you;
An' if sometimes our conduck isn't all your fancy paints,
Why, single men in barricks don't grow into plaster saints;
    While it's Tommy this, an' Tommy that, an' "Tommy, fall be'ind",
    But it's "Please to walk in front, sir", when there's trouble in the wind,
    There's trouble in the wind, my boys, there's trouble in the wind,
    O it's "Please to walk in front, sir", when there's trouble in the wind.

You talk o' better food for us, an' schools, an' fires, an' all:
We'll wait for extry rations if you treat us rational.
Don't mess about the cook-room slops, but prove it to our face
The Widow's Uniform is not the soldier-man's disgrace.
    For it's Tommy this, an' Tommy that, an' "Chuck him out, the brute!"
    But it's "Saviour of 'is country" when the guns begin to shoot;
    An' it's Tommy this, an' Tommy that, an' anything you please;
    An' Tommy ain't a bloomin' fool — you bet that Tommy sees!

Soldier, Soldier

Another of the Barrack Room Ballads, *this poem is written from the perspective of a girl hopefully and fearfully waiting for the return of her "true love" from the battlefield. Inquiring of each returning soldier about his whereabouts and wellbeing, she is hit with a dose of sad reality and frank advice. The poem shows that great pain can be dealt within poetry and that poetry does not have to be "pie in the sky" or "feel good" platitudes, but can be earthy, factual, and vividly clear.*

— *R.W.*

"Soldier, soldier come from the wars,
Why don't you march with my true love?"
"We're fresh from off the ship an' 'e's maybe give the slip,
An' you'd best go look for a new love."

    New love! True love!
    Best go look for a new love,
    The dead they cannot rise, an' you'd better dry your eyes,
    An' you'd best go look for a new love.

"Soldier, soldier come from the wars,
What did you see o' my true love?"
"I seed 'im serve the Queen in a suit o' rifle-green,
An' you'd best go look for a new love."

"Soldier, soldier come from the wars,
Did ye see no more o' my true love?"
"I seed 'im runnin' by when the shots begun to fly —
But you'd best go look for a new love."

"Soldier, soldier come from the wars,
Did aught take 'arm to my true love?"

"I couldn't see the fight, for the smoke it lay so white —
An' you'd best go look for a new love."

"Soldier, soldier come from the wars,
I'll up an' tend to my true love!"
"'E's lying on the dead with a bullet through 'is 'ead,
An' you'd best go look for a new love."

"Soldier, soldier come from the wars,
I'll down an' die with my true love!"
"The pit we dug'll 'ide 'im an' the twenty men beside 'im —
An' you'd best go look for a new love."

"Soldier, soldier come from the wars,
Do you bring no sign from my true love?"
"I bring a lock of 'air that 'e allus used to wear,
An' you'd best go look for a new love."

"Soldier, soldier come from the wars,
O then I know it's true I've lost my true love!"
"An' I tell you truth again — when you've lost the feel o' pain
You'd best take me for your true love."

> True love! New love!
> Best take 'im for a new love,
> The dead they cannot rise, an' you'd better dry your eyes,
> An' you'd best take 'im for your true love.

Tomlinson

Tomlinson is not a poem from which we should seek to gain any theological insight, whether on the nature and relationships of Heaven and Hell, or the means by which one might gain entrance into either of those places. Nevertheless, Tomlinson *contains many truths of the Christian life and of the human condition as such.*

In the story, a wealthy Englishman dies, and his spirit is interviewed, first by St. Peter at the gates of Heaven, then by Satan at the entrance to Hell. These interviews find him out as a man with no soul of his own, in that he has never thought an original thought, nor done an original deed, but has all his life lived vicariously through the thoughts and deeds of others: among them are Leo Tolstoy, Henrik Ibsen, and the Marquis de Sade.

Found innocent of sufficient virtue or vice to be granted entrance into eiher heaven or hell, Tomlinson is returned posthaste to his home in Berkeley Square and admonished to live on his own behalf thenceforth.

— D.G.

Now Tomlinson gave up the ghost in his house in Berkeley Square,
And a Spirit came to his bedside and gripped him by the hair —
A Spirit gripped him by the hair and carried him far away,
Till he heard as the roar of a rain-fed ford the roar of the Milky Way:
Till he heard the roar of the Milky Way die down and drone and cease,
And they came to the Gate within the Wall where Peter holds the keys.
"Stand up, stand up now, Tomlinson, and answer loud and high
The good that ye did for the sake of men or ever ye came to die —
The good that ye did for the sake of men in little earth so lone!"
And the naked soul of Tomlinson grew white as a rain-washed bone.
"O I have a friend on earth," he said, "that was my priest and guide,
And well would he answer all for me if he were by my side."
— "For that ye strove in neighbour-love it shall be written fair,
But now ye wait at Heaven's Gate and not in Berkeley Square:
Though we called your friend from his bed this night, he could not speak for you,

For the race is run by one and one and never by two and two."
Then Tomlinson looked up and down, and little gain was there,
For the naked stars grinned overhead, and he saw that his soul was bare:
The Wind that blows between the worlds, it cut him like a knife,
And Tomlinson took up his tale and spoke of his good in life.
"This I have read in a book," he said, "and that was told to me,
And this I have thought that another man thought of a Prince in Muscovy."
The good souls flocked like homing doves and bade him clear the path,
And Peter twirled the jangling keys in weariness and wrath.
"Ye have read, ye have heard, ye have thought," he said, "and the tale is yet to run:
By the worth of the body that once ye had, give answer — what ha' ye done?"
Then Tomlinson looked back and forth, and little good it bore,
For the Darkness stayed at his shoulder-blade and Heaven's Gate before: —
"O this I have felt, and this I have guessed, and this I have heard men say,
And this they wrote that another man wrote of a carl in Norroway."
— "Ye have read, ye have felt, ye have guessed, good lack! Ye have hampered
              Heaven's Gate;
There's little room between the stars in idleness to prate!
O none may reach by hired speech of neighbour, priest, and kin
Through borrowed deed to God's good meed that lies so fair within;
Get hence, get hence to the Lord of Wrong, for doom has yet to run,
And…the faith that ye share with Berkeley Square uphold you, Tomlinson!"

. . . . .

The Spirit gripped him by the hair, and sun by sun they fell
Till they came to the belt of Naughty Stars that rim the mouth of Hell:
The first are red with pride and wrath, the next are white with pain,
But the third are black with clinkered sin that cannot burn again:
They may hold their path, they may leave their path, with never a soul to mark,
They may burn or freeze, but they must not cease in the Scorn of the Outer Dark.
The Wind that blows between the worlds, it nipped him to the bone,
And he yearned to the flare of Hell-Gate there as the light of his own hearth stone.
The Devil he sat behind the bars, where the desperate legions drew,

But he caught the hasting Tomlinson and would not let him through.
"Wot ye the price of good pit-coal that I must pay?" said he,
"That ye rank yoursel' so fit for Hell and ask no leave of me?
I am all o'er-sib to Adam's breed that ye should give me scorn,
For I strove with God for your First Father the day that he was born.
Sit down, sit down upon the slag, and answer loud and high
The harm that ye did to the Sons of Men or ever you came to die."
And Tomlinson looked up and up, and saw against the night
The belly of a tortured star blood-red in Hell-Mouth light;
And Tomlinson looked down and down, and saw beneath his feet
The frontlet of a tortured star milk-white in Hell-Mouth heat.
"O I had a love on earth," said he, "that kissed me to my fall,
And if ye would call my love to me I know she would answer all."
— "All that ye did in love forbid it shall be written fair,
But now ye wait at Hell-Mouth Gate and not in Berkeley Square:
Though we whistled your love from her bed to-night, I trow she would not run,
For the sin ye do by two and two ye must pay for one by one!"
The Wind that blows between the worlds, it cut him like a knife,
And Tomlinson took up the tale and spoke of his sin in life: —
"Once I ha' laughed at the power of Love and twice at the grip of the Grave,
And thrice I ha' patted my God on the head that men might call me brave."
The Devil he blew on a brandered soul and set it aside to cool: —
"Do ye think I would waste my good pit-coal on the hide of a brain-sick fool?
I see no worth in the hobnailed mirth or the jolthead jest ye did
That I should waken my gentlemen that are sleeping three on a grid."
Then Tomlinson looked back and forth, and there was little grace,
For Hell-Gate filled the houseless Soul with the Fear of Naked Space.
"Nay, this I ha' heard," quo' Tomlinson, "and this was noised abroad,
And this I ha' got from a Belgian book on the word of a dead French lord."
— "Ye ha' heard, ye ha' read, ye ha' got, good lack! and the tale begins afresh —
Have ye sinned one sin for the pride o' the eye or the sinful lust of the flesh?"
Then Tomlinson he gripped the bars and yammered, "Let me in —
For I mind that I borrowed my neighbour's wife to sin the deadly sin."
The Devil he grinned behind the bars, and banked the fires high:

"Did ye read of that sin in a book?" said he; and Tomlinson said, "Ay!"
The Devil he blew upon his nails, and the little devils ran,
And he said: "Go husk this whimpering thief that comes in the guise of a man:
Winnow him out 'twixt star and star, and sieve his proper worth:
There's sore decline in Adam's line if this be spawn of earth."
Empusa's crew, so naked-new they may not face the fire,
But weep that they bin too small to sin to the height of their desire,
Over the coal they chased the Soul, and racked it all abroad,
As children rifle a caddis-case or the raven's foolish hoard.
And back they came with the tattered Thing, as children after play,
And they said: "The soul that he got from God he has bartered clean away.
We have threshed a stook of print and book, and winnowed a chattering wind
And many a soul wherefrom he stole, but his we cannot find:
We have handled him, we have dandled him, we have seared him to the bone,
And sure if tooth and nail show truth he has no soul of his own."
The Devil he bowed his head on his breast and rumbled deep and low: —
"I'm all o'er-sib to Adam's breed that I should bid him go.
Yet close we lie, and deep we lie, and if I gave him place,
My gentlemen that are so proud would flout me to my face;
They'd call my house a common stews and me a careless host,
And — I would not anger my gentlemen for the sake of a shiftless ghost."
The Devil he looked at the mangled Soul that prayed to feel the flame,
And he thought of Holy Charity, but he thought of his own good name: —
"Now ye could haste my coal to waste, and sit ye down to fry:
Did ye think of that theft for yourself?" said he; and Tomlinson said, "Ay!"
The Devil he blew an outward breath, for his heart was free from care: —
"Ye have scarce the soul of a louse," he said, "but the roots of sin are there,
And for that sin should ye come in were I the lord alone.
But sinful pride has rule inside — and mightier than my own.
Honour and Wit, fore-damned they sit, to each his priest and whore:
Nay, scarce I dare myself go there, and you they'd torture sore.
Ye are neither spirit nor spirk," he said; "ye are neither book nor brute —
Go, get ye back to the flesh again for the sake of Man's repute.
I'm all o'er-sib to Adam's breed that I should mock your pain,

But look that ye win to worthier sin ere ye come back again.
Get hence, the hearse is at your door — the grim black stallions wait —
They bear your clay to place to-day. Speed, lest ye come too late!
Go back to Earth with a lip unsealed — go back with an open eye,
And carry my word to the Sons of Men or ever ye come to die:
That the sin they do by two and two they must pay for one by one —
And... the God that you took from a printed book be with you, Tomlinson!"

Boots

It is easy to see that Kipling admired military life and deeply felt the burdens of the soldier (though he never personally served in the military). From 1900-1902 Kipling wrote the Service Songs - South African War. *He simply called one of the poems of this age,* Boots, *describing the everyday woes of the infantryman. Kipling had a way of boiling life down to the little things, which often become the biggest frustrations of day-to-day life. It is reported that this poem is used in the US Navy's "Survival, Evasion, Resistance, and Escape" (SERE) training to psychologically prepare sailors for the rigors of war.*

   Boots *is a fine display of the manner in which Kipling used rhythm as much as rhyme to communicate. Many of Kipling's poems do not clearly communicate the message until the rhythm is found.*

—R.W.

WE'RE foot—slog—slog—slog—sloggin' over Africa!
Foot—foot—foot—foot—sloggin' over Africa—
(Boots—boots—boots—boots—movin' up and down again!)
   There's no discharge in the war!

Seven—six—eleven—five—nine-an'-twenty mile to-day—
Four—eleven—seventeen—thirty-two the day before—
(Boots—boots—boots—boots—movin' up and down again!)
   There's no discharge in the war!

Don't—don't—don't—don't—look at what's in front of you.
(Boots—boots—boots—boots—movin' up an' down again!)
Men—men—men—men—men go mad with watchin' 'em,
   And there's no discharge in the war!

Try—try—try—try—to think o' something different—
Oh—my—God—keep—me from goin' lunatic!

(Boots—boots—boots—boots—movin' up an' down again!)
      There's no discharge in the war!

Count—count—count—count—the bullets in the bandoliers.
If—your—eyes—drop—they will get atop o' you
(Boots—boots—boots—boots—movin' up and down again!)
      There's no discharge in the war!

We—can—stick—out—'unger, thirst, an' weariness,
But—not—not—not—not the chronic sight of 'em—
Boots—boots—boots—boots—movin' up an' down again!
      An' there's no discharge in the war!

'Tain't—so—bad—by—day because o' company,
But—night—brings—long—strings—o' forty thousand million
Boots—boots—boots—boots—movin' up an' down again.
      There's no discharge in the war!

I—'ave—marched—six—weeks in 'Ell an' certify
It—is—not—fire—devils—dark or anything,
But boots—boots—boots—boots—movin' up an' down again,
      An' there's no discharge in the war!

Bill 'Awkins

Kipling's Barrak Room Ballads II, *written from 1892-1896, included the short poem* Bill 'Awkins. *The poem is a conversation between two strangers: one looking for Bill, though he doesn't know him personally; the other knows Bill personally and does not recommend looking for him!*

The poem shows Kipling's love of the cockney accent, which he often conveyed in print with the use of apostrophes for the silent 'H' ('Awkins rather than Hawkins).

The message of the poem: sometimes it's easier to face the enemy with strength when we have not actually seen the enemy!

—*R.W.*

"'As anybody seen Bill 'Awkins?"
   "Now 'ow in the devil would I know?"
"'E's taken my girl out walkin',
   An' I've got to tell 'im so —
     Gawd — bless — 'im!
   I've got to tell 'im so."

"D'yer know what 'e's like, Bill 'Awkins?"
   "Now what in the devil would I care?"
"'E's the livin', breathin' image of an organ-grinder's monkey,
   With a pound of grease in 'is 'air —
     Gawd — bless — 'im!
   An' a pound o' grease in 'is 'air."

"An' s'pose you met Bill 'Awkins,
   Now what in the devil 'ud ye do?"
"I'd open 'is cheek to 'is chin-strap buckle,
   An' bung up 'is both eyes, too —
     Gawd — bless — 'im!
   An bung up 'is both eyes, too!"

"Look 'ere, where 'e comes, Bill 'Awkins!
  Now, what in the devil will you say?"
"It isn't fit an' proper to be fightin' on a Sunday,
  So I'll pass 'im the time o' day —
    Gawd — bless — 'im!
  I'll pass 'im the time o' day!"

En-dor

Published in 1919, in a collection of verse called The Years Between, *Kipling speaks against a rising public interest in spiritualism, or communication with the dead, in the wake of the Great War. Having lost his own son to that war, the poet was no doubt aware of that impulse, but he directs the bereaved to the story of Saul, who commissioned the witch of En-dor to summon the spirit of the prophet Samuel, with grievous results.*

— D.G.

> "Behold there is a woman that hath
> a familiar spirit at En-dor."
> I. Samuel 28:7.

The road to En-dor is easy to tread
  For Mother or yearning Wife.
There, it is sure, we shall meet our Dead
  As they were even in life.
Earth has not dreamed of the blessing in store
For desolate hearts on the road to En-dor.

Whispers shall comfort us out of the dark—
  Hands—ah God!—that we knew!
Visions and voices —look and hark!—
  Shall prove that the tale is true,
An that those who have passed to the further shore
May' be hailed—at a price—on the road to En-dor.

But they are so deep in their new eclipse
  Nothing they say can reach,
Unless it be uttered by alien lips
  And framed in a stranger's speech.
The son must send word to the mother that bore,
'Through an hireling's mouth. 'Tis the rule of En-dor.

And not for nothing these gifts are shown
  By such as delight our dead.
They must twitch and stiffen and slaver and groan
  Ere the eyes are set in the head,
And the voice from the belly begins. Therefore,
We pay them a wage where they ply at En-dor.

Even so, we have need of faith
  And patience to follow the clue.
Often, at first, what the dear one saith
  Is babble, or jest, or untrue.
(Lying spirits perplex us sore
Till our loves—and their lives—are well-known at
    En-dor). . . .

Oh the road to En-dor is the oldest road
  And the craziest road of all!
Straight it runs to the Witch's abode,
  As it did in the days of Saul,
And nothing has changed of the sorrow in store
For such as go down on the road to En-dor!

My Boy Jack

This poem was written in 1915, the same year that John Kipling fell in battle at Loos in Normandy. Although it is not specifically about John, and was published with a story about the naval engagement at Jutland, the heartbreak of the grieving father screams from every line.

— D. G.

"Have you news of my boy Jack?"
Not this tide.
"When d'you think that he'll come back?"
Not with this wind blowing, and this tide.

"Has any one else had word of him?"
Not this tide.
For what is sunk will hardly swim,
Not with this wind blowing, and this tide.

"Oh, dear, what comfort can I find?"
None this tide,
Nor any tide,
Except he did not shame his kind—
Not even with that wind blowing, and that tide.

Then hold your head up all the more,
This tide,
And every tide;
Because he was the son you bore,
And gave to that wind blowing and that tide.

Cold Iron

The imagery and wording of this 1909 poem ring straight from the Bible and from Christian Europe. Kipling presents to us the arrogance of man in his own might, the rebellion that arrogance breeds, and the humiliation of defeat. But then, he shows us the love of Christ as He forgives the vanquished rebel and restores him to his place, even against the fallen man's protestations. Lastly, he shows us the repentant heart of the rebellious Baron, submitted to his Lord.

— D.G.

Gold is for the mistress — silver for the maid —
Copper for the craftsman cunning at his trade."
"Good!" said the Baron, sitting in his hall,
"But Iron — Cold Iron — is master of them all."

So he made rebellion 'gainst the King his liege,
Camped before his citadel and summoned it to siege.
"Nay!" said the cannoneer on the castle wall,
"But Iron — Cold Iron — shall be master of you all!"

Woe for the Baron and his knights so strong,
When the cruel cannon-balls laid 'em all along;
He was taken prisoner, he was cast in thrall,
And Iron — Cold Iron — was master of it all!

Yet his King spake kindly (ah, how kind a Lord!)
"What if I release thee now and give thee back thy sword?"
"Nay!" said the Baron, "mock not at my fall,
For Iron — Cold Iron — is master of men all."

"Tears are for the craven, prayers are for the clown —
Halters for the silly neck that cannot keep a crown."

"As my loss is grievous, so my hope is small,
For Iron — Cold Iron — must be master of men all!"

Yet his King made answer (few such Kings there be!)
"Here is Bread and here is Wine — sit and sup with me.
Eat and drink in Mary's Name, the whiles I do recall
How Iron — Cold Iron — can be master of men all!"

He took the Wine and blessed it. He blessed and brake the Bread.
With His own Hands He served Them, and presently He said:
"See! These Hands they pierced with nails, outside My city wall,
Show Iron — Cold Iron — to be master of men all."

"Wounds are for the desperate, blows are for the strong.
Balm and oil for weary hearts all cut and bruised with wrong.
I forgive thy treason — I redeem thy fall —
For Iron — Cold Iron — must be master of men all!"

"Crowns are for the valiant — sceptres for the bold!
Thrones and powers for mighty men who dare to take and hold!"
"Nay!" said the Baron, kneeling in his hall,
"But Iron — Cold Iron — is master of men all!
Iron out of Calvary is master of men all!"

Recessional

Kipling wrote Recessional *in 1897, not long after bringing his family back to England from America. Here we see a deep sense of foreboding for the future of his beloved British Empire — a word of warning not to take for granted the achievements of previous generations.*

— D.G.

God of our fathers, known of old —
  Lord of our far-flung battle line —
Beneath whose awful hand we hold
  Dominion over palm and pine —
Lord God of Hosts, be with us yet,
Lest we forget — lest we forget!

The tumult and the shouting dies —
  The Captains and the Kings depart —
Still stands Thine ancient sacrifice,
  An humble and a contrite heart.
Lord God of Hosts, be with us yet,
Lest we forget — lest we forget!

Far-called our navies melt away —
  On dune and headland sinks the fire —
Lo, all our pomp of yesterday
  Is one with Nineveh and Tyre!
Judge of the Nations, spare us yet,
Lest we forget — lest we forget!

If, drunk with sight of power, we loose
  Wild tongues that have not Thee in awe —
Such boastings as the Gentiles use,

Or lesser breeds without the Law —
Lord God of Hosts, be with us yet,
Lest we forget — lest we forget!

For heathen heart that puts her trust
  In reeking tube and iron shard —
All valiant dust that builds on dust,
  And guarding calls not Thee to guard.
For frantic boast and foolish word,
Thy Mercy on Thy People, Lord!
              Amen.

www.ingramcontent.com/pod-product-compliance
Lightning Source LLC
Chambersburg PA
CBHW071755080526
44588CB00013B/2239